SPILLING OPEN

the Art of Becoming Yourself.

SABRINA ward HARRison

NEW WORLD LIBRARY

New World Library
Novato, California

New WORLD Library
14 Pamaron Way
NOVATO, CA 94949

Copyright © 1999 Sabrina Ward Harrison

Pre-Press and Color Separations, Alphadigaraphics, NOVATO CA

Photography, ART, and DesibN: Sabrina Ward Harrison

EDITORIAL: Becky BENenaTE

LIBRARY OF Congress-in-publication Data

Harrison, Sabrina WARD.
Spilling Open: the art of becoming yourself / Sabrina Ward Harrison.
       P   cm.
    ISBN 1-57731-044-6 (alk paper)
    1 Self-perception. 2. Self-Acceptance. 3. Harrison, Sabrina Ward — Diaries.

    I. Title.
    BF697.5.S43H37 1999
    158.1—dc21

         First printing, February 1999
         Publishers Group West
         10 9 8 7 6 5 4 3 2 1

A FOREWORD. BY SARK
BACKWARD. FOURWORD. FOUR WORDS:

THIS IS WHAT IS

SABRINA IS A luminous mystery,
A CAROUSEL of FeeLiNGS, lumps
and Discoveries.

 IF you could lie Down with
Her JournALS, you would see Genius.
 THAT Genius is in THiS BOOK.
 Yes she is (YOUNG) THank
GOD ÷ We miGHT Get THAT MuCH
More From/of Her.
 WHen I reaD This BOOK, I AM
reminDeD of illuMinated Manuscripts,

"Deep tALKiNG" FroM AFriCA, sweet spilling teA and FrAGrant BedSHeets.

Your SOUL will AWAKeN aND you MAY FiND your BeD Flying to rAre plAces AT NiGHT.

Do it.

Get out of your NiGHTGowN aND lie NAKeD iN MOONLiGHT.

See throVGH SABrina eyes.

I ASSure you of A NoUrishing voyAGe. THere Are words aND pictures Here thAT Move us to Cry aND FLOAT siMULTaneoVsly.

Dive Deep.

Be SurpriSeD By this Book aND the KiNDreD Spirit you will FiND iNSiDe.

Be ASSureD of iNveNtions, journeys, aND MeSSAGes.

SHe is SHAriNG Her reAL Self Here aND letting us see iNSiDe. I celeBrAte Her SOUL aND All thAT it contaiNs.

love, SARK

introduction

THE GREAT AMERICAN POET WALT WHITMAN said that there is a time we must "WASH the gum FROM OUR eyes and DRESS ourselves FOR THE DAZZLE of the Light." HE looked at men and women struggling WITH THEIR lives and SAID,

"Long HAVE you timidly WADED holding A plank by the SHORE, now I will you to BE A bold SWIMMER, to jump off into the Midst of the SEA, rise again, NOD to me, SHOUT! and laughingly DASH WITH your HAIR."

in her grown up clothing?

1 2 3 4 5 6 7 8 9 10

IM Feeling Rather → DISHEVELED,
and slightly crooked
(I SEEM to BE SEEPING out AT THE EDGES.)
I am Sabrina WARD HARRISON
I am twenty One.

THIS IS
MY BOOK.

I OFTEN FEEL AN OVERWELMING PRESSURE TO
"Have It all together"
WHAT IS "It"?
2 3 4 5 8 9 0
I FEEL YOUng.   I AM young

childrens BOOK author and Artist → maurice SENDAK
DESCRIBED his creative process
as A "DESCENT into LimBO"
→ THIS DESCRIBES my ENTIRE LIFE LATELY

THE MORE I LOOK ArOUnd and LisTEN
→ I REALIZE that i'm not alone.

full

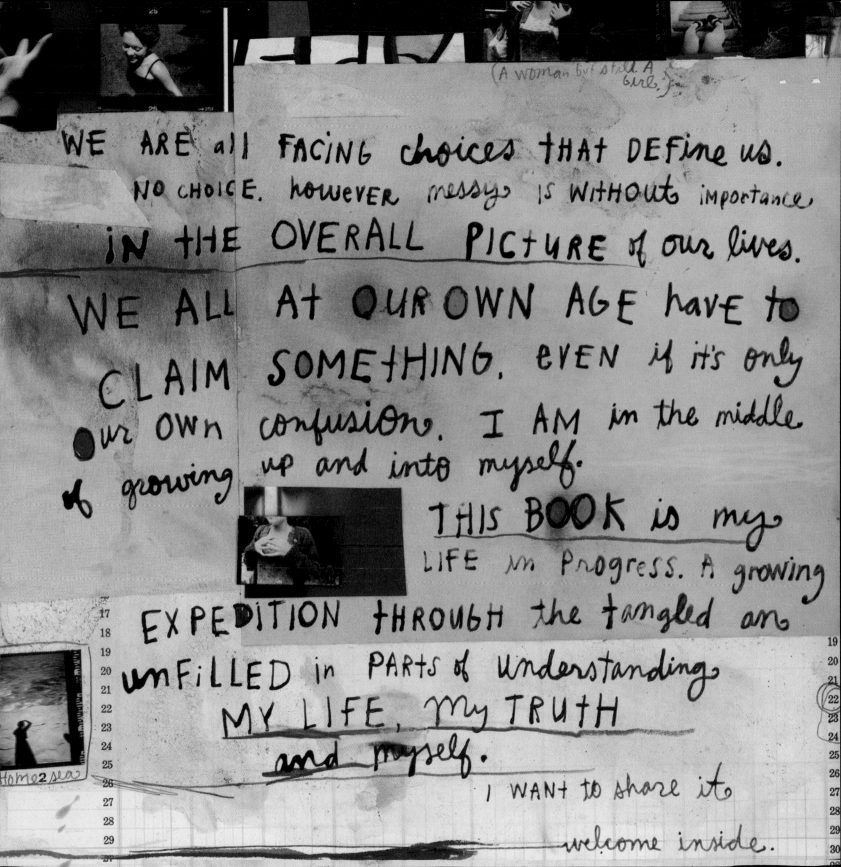

(A woman but still A girl.)

WE ARE all FACING choices THAT DEFine us.
NO CHOICE. however messy IS WITHOUT importance.
iN THE OVERALL PICTURE of our lives.
WE ALL AT OUR OWN AGE have to
CLAIM SOMETHING. even if it's only
our own confusion. I AM in the middle
of growing up and into myself.
THIS BOOK is my
LIFE in Progress. A growing
EXPEDITION THROUGH the tangled an
unFILLED in PARts of Understanding
MY LIFE, MY TRUTH
and myself.

i WANT to share it

welcome inside.

Home2sea

17
18
19
20
21
22
23
24
25
26
27
28
29

19
20
21
22
23
24
25
26
27
28
29
30

THE BASIC. THE. ANGRY. THE SAD. the LOST.
THE. WONdering. the small One.
The Dreamer. ~~THE BELIEVER.~~
THE YOUNG. THE BRAVE.
THE WEAK. the strong.
THE ALone. The together.
THE SAFE. the unexpected.
the annoying. the insecure. the waiting.
THE WISHER. THE glowing.
the understANDing? THE SCARED.
tHE HOLDING BACK. the Letting GO.
tHE STRUe and the QUESTION.
THE ME I KNOW. the me I DONT

I have Been feeling so BLANK
and full OF MUTED tones.
I feel just sort of Beige.
I've been stuck in MUCK.
YESTERDAY I got MY HAIR CUT
so SHORT that WHEN I WENT
to SCHOOL CHRISTOPHER SAID
I looked like AN eNGLISH school BOY
SO THAT DIDN't HELP.
my face feels wide
and naked.
(...it just looked so good in the magazine

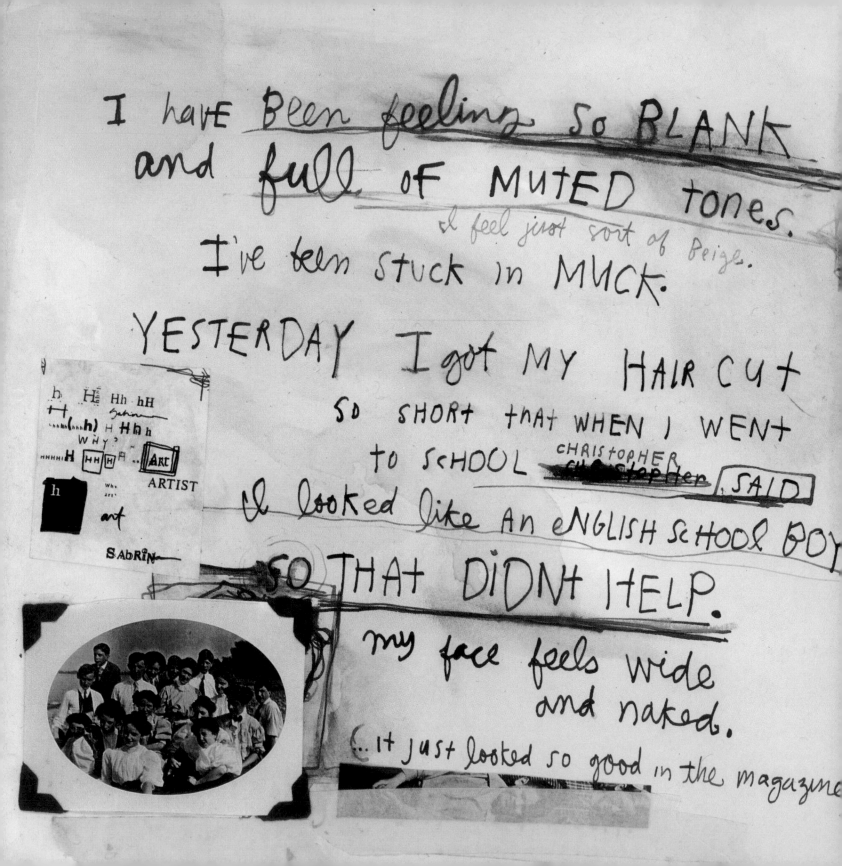

h Hʰ Hh hH
H Sabrina
(h) H Hh h
WHY?
HHHHhH H HH H Art
ARTIST
h
art
SABRINA

I CATCH Myself trying to
COVER UP the Parts of myself that I dont accept.
It's like A MASK.
I USE my Long Black skirts
to cover my legs that
Feel THick sometimes

cover 'up
HIGH SHOES

I wear my clunky black shoes
to GIVE ME SOLID ground
and A BIT more HIGHT
(I usually trip a lot more though)
I put MAKE-UP ON
that Attempts to look like
I DONT have make-up on
just to COVER any
SHADOWS OF ACNE.
WHY?

IF I WANT to BE ACCEPTED AND LOVED
as is. WITHOUT the
'EXtrA Attachments'

THIGHS
OH...THE WORRIES OF thighs...
thighs thighs.

why do I keep it up?
this Bewilders me

Make up
OWN eM'.

mys
★ FEAR of wHAt is
left 'under it all
isnt enough.

4 WHO do I wear a mask FOR today?

I tHInk masks say, "APPROVE me"

"ACCEPt me" "LOVE me."

MASKS dont SAY ⟶ tHis IS ME as is

as I reatly AM.

★ so WHAT Am I witHout the masks? WHAT am I FROM the inside OUt?

2 22 22 % (3) 24

I Never Passed ALgebRA.

2 I CAN+ SPELL MucH   i don't really Believe in algebra. £10

I dont OWN drawers

⟶ I HAD BAD ACNE. I have scars.

IM not SLICK At GAMES involving BAlls being tHrowN or kicked towards me

4

I FEEL stumpy in SWEAtPANts (especially ones with pOckets)

MASKS
2 long skirts
3 cover up
high shoes
4 eye liners

So much of my growing up has been spent trying to figure out WHO I am and ~~accept~~ accept WHO I am

and perhaps even love WHO I AM.

BODY.

unFORtunatly I have noticed that I SPEND A LOt of time comparing myself to other young WOMEN my AGE, WAtching For traits they possess that I feel I lack.

It's very EXHAUSTING.

BETTER

★ THE SHIRT Around THE WAist trick...

OH to Look 'thinner.'

sleeping up to look "casual" for a boy.

1. long Legs
2. clear skin "RADIANt"
3. thick HAIR
4. the right "wake up and go look"

DON'T QUIT ON YOURSELF.

our BODIES make us WORRY.

★ awkward (REAL) covering up ourselves

legs and FRECKLES.

legs

"really get ready" THE GETTING READY TIME, to look like you didn't

★ Deadly INSECURITIES... BE YOURSELF ALL WAYS."

But I seem to keep COMPARING and DESIRING ("NEEDING") MORE or WANTING Less.

WHEN DO I STOP and BE SABRINA the way I am?

when do I stop and believe that I AM ENOUGH as I am?

WITH all the PARTS of me that feel 'too small' or 'too Lumpy' or "too Quiet" or not 'edgy' or 'too Deep Feeling; TOO TOO TOO too.

I MUST Ask myself "WHAT am I trying to Be that I already AM?"

IF I don't love those parts of me, the tucked in SUCKED in Silent PARTS..

I think it will Be a very SAD journey. and A PATHETIC WASTE of TIME.

"If you're not yourself WHO WILL BE?"

I DON'T HAVE 10 foot long Legs.

(and I also CAN't draw Feet

COVER UP

It's shocking how HARD I AM on myself. why?

AMANDA

THE truth is WE All ACHE.
WE All HAVE GROWING PAINS
and wonder if WE ARE
OKAY and enough + loved.
THE thing is — WE ARE.
REALLY.
Without the silver shoes
and lepord print sheets.
WE ARE ENOUGH Without
all THE things WE Buy,
to make us much more
than WE are or need to Be
WE ARE simple
and complex
and RARE
as is.

WHO
DO
YOU
let in?

I struggle with this with my art + journals—always wanting to become better + better thinking it will make me MORE somehow — fill the places that are awkward + unsure. to cover up those parts with color + pictures. I hope to become braver at being bare more + let myown simple LOVE in towards myself that loves the fumbling unsure pieces of me... the sameway the BOLD daring parts want to glow as well. → But those parts alone arnt the answer And they certainly are just a small part of me.

LOOKING BACK on this YEAR I can see HOW
I HAVE caused MUCH OF MY OWN SUFFERING
FOR REASONS of PRIDE, ego and INSECURITY (what is left unsaid)
Pain and ache are felt IN THE unexpressed
PARTS of My life → WHEN I didn't speak up, spill open
and BE
truely WHO
I AM.

i learn and re-learn
that Silence
DOESN'T PROTECT [ME]
an unexpressed life is very PAINFUL to
myself and those I LOVE.

DON'T LOVE HALFWAY

I am LEARNING
that loving
all the way
can ache + sting, but loving HALFWAY

LOVED.

doesn't keep me SAFE. it leaves
ME WITH SADNESS and
A HOPE
that could never
LIVE OUT LOUD.

22
2268 09
8922
NAME

With my freckles
and messy HAIR,
Brused knee
AND chapped Lips —
THis morning
I AM splendidly
Imperfect and alive.
another BATH it
will Be.

short HAIR is gooD.

Bless the Mess.

freckles

Mom and I were WALKING on the BEACH and I WAS explaining to her HOW I wanted to "GET OVER all my INSECURITIES" and "La La...La"...

and she looked at me and said "SABRINA, does anyone really feel good about themselves for MORE THAN 5 Minutes?"

we both laughed. I was relieaved to know she felt that way because she seems

M.M.

SO graceful, calm and Beautiful, which she is.. but also full of so much more. avestions, doubts + WONDER. I think that if we can aim for just five minutes a day of complete Acceptance of ourselves, we are doing very well!

BELONG to yourself.

seaside

HOW ONE lives as a PRIVATE PERSON is INTIMATELY bound INTO THE WORK. At some POINT I Believe ONE HAS TO stop HOLDING back For FEAR Of Alienating some IMAGINARY reADER or real ~~real~~ RELATIVE or FRIEND, and COME out with personal TRUTH. If we ArE to understand THE Human condition, and if we are to accept OURSELVES in all the complexity, Self DOUBT, extravagance of feeling GUILT JOY the slow Freeing of the self to its full capacity For Action and creation BOTH as Human Being, and AS Artist, WE HAVE to know All WE CAN ABOut eachOTHER and we have to Be willing to GO NAKED." MAY SARTON.

WORK Like you, 1 2 3
DONt need THE money

LoVe like YOU'VE
LoVE   yes ★
NEVER BEEN
HURt
DANCE like no
ONE IS WATCHING

— Kathy Mattea

Today was just one of THOSE DAYS
I woke up wanting to go to Italy by CAR.
Perhaps if I really drove fast enough I might
CATCH AIR to FLORENCE
instead of Typography class this morning

Sometimes I forget about the magic.
like the moon and red leaves and HOW
the apples grow AGAIN and AGAIN
Outside my windows.
Life HAS felt overwelming lately

Today in class I had to climb
under the desks during the ~~on~~ → critique
to GET a GRIP of my "meish-ness" (thats what megan
to find myself again... I don't calls being all yourself)
think anyone noticed me DISAPPEAR.
I can feel so suffocated at school —
WATCHING + THINKING + WONDERING
~~how~~ I fit - in the world...
HOW it can look so easy.
"JUST RELAX"

WOULD I be relaxed
u IN ITALY, spinning under deep night skies?
perhaps... BUT NOW I AM here,
        in BERKELEY California.
I WANt TO GROW COMFORTABLE
with myself HERE NOW.

        so I took off my black skirt
    and BIG Clunky SHOES
I put on overalls and got a slurpie FrOm
    7-11 - turned on TRACY CHAPMAN
    WASHED the makeup off my face,
    And became the ME that I love
    and know the
            BEST.

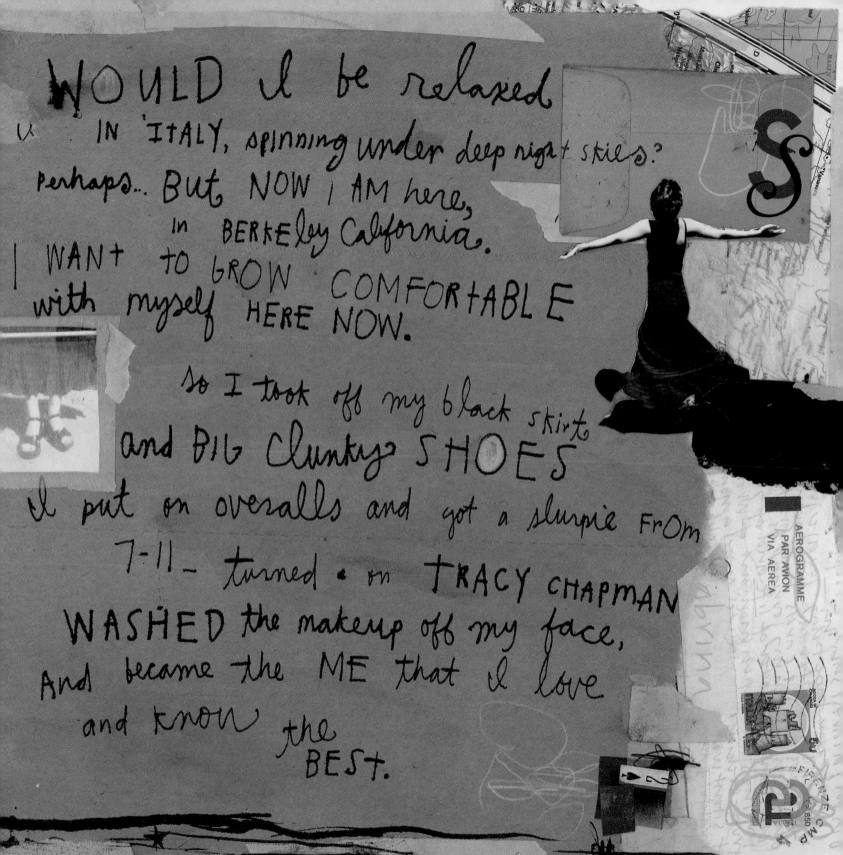

"I certainly DO Not HOpe to ALTER the world. PerHAPS I CAN PUt IT BEST by sayen I HOPE to alter MyOWN VISION of THE WORLD

I WANT TO ⟶ BE MORE and MORE mySELF

AS RIDICULOUS as tHAt may SOUNd."

HENRy miller

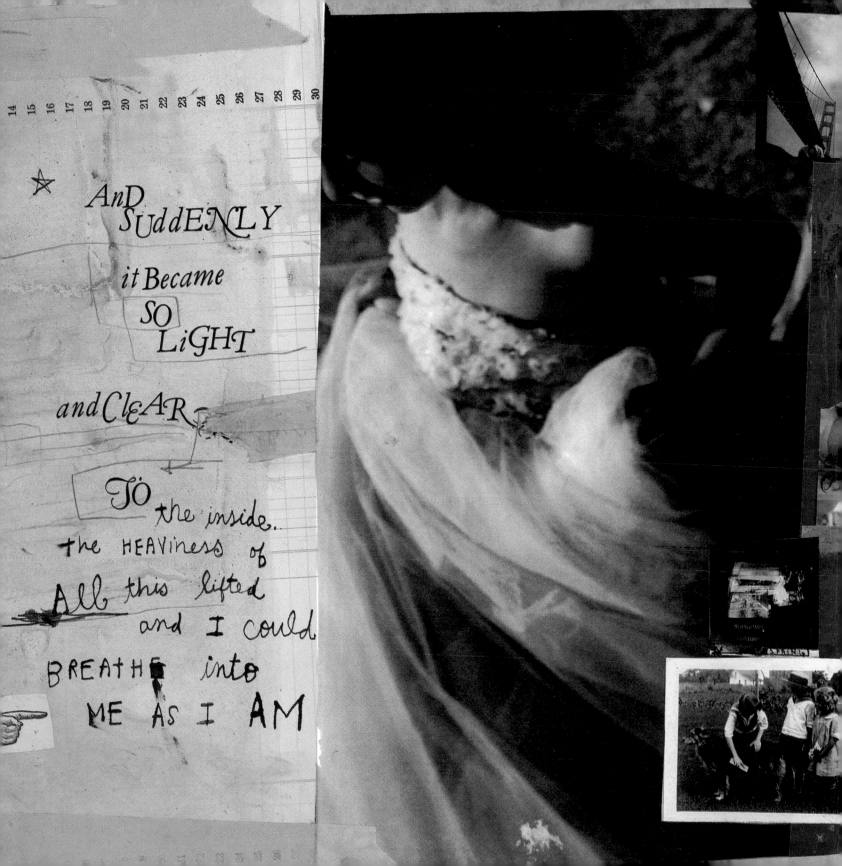

14 15 16 17 18 19 20 21 22 23 24 25 26 27 28 29 30

AnD
SuddENLY

it Became
SO
LiGHT

and ClEAR

To the inside..
the HEAViness of
All this lifted
and I could
BREATHE into
ME AS I AM

6

MY FRIEND SUSAN ALWAYS REMINDS
ME THAT THE ULTIMATE GOAL IS
RADICAL SELF ACCEPTANCE.
get into who you are.

THAT IS WHAT INSPIRED ME SO MUCH
BOUT MEETING the PHOTOGRAPHER,
ELIZABETH SUNDAY. SHE SAID:

"I BELIEVE in myself. I BELIEVE
IN MY VISION, my life, MY TALENT,
my ART. MORE THAN anyone.
NO ONE CAN TAKE THAT AWAY
FROM ME"...
i THINK when i can get to
that place of self acceptance
AND A sence OF CALM assurance

IN WHO I GENUINELY AM - If I CAN
BElieve in WHO I AM, WHAT I
NEED, WHAT I deserve
AND what I MUST
EXPRESS
then I can
Let GO of the struggle
of self acceptance BASED ON
'THEIR' approval of my Beauty,
BOOBs, THIGHS,
or SKETCHBOOKS
I WILL DARE to do just WHAT I do,
Be Just WHAT I AM
and dance WHENever I want
TO

EVERY girl is a princess. that's a fact. No matter how **slender,** pretty, smart, popular **or nice.** They are all Royalty, a princess in themselfs. If they beLive, **they can** be a pri-

ncess if they look into their **heart** and if they think they are too poor, too u- gly **or** 7040 not smart, **they** are WRONG.

TO: Sabrina **FROM!** Meagam

overwelmed with nothing

WORRY

GIVE

RICA

Katsina

Kano

Koduna

G E R I

Growing

growing

BARE.

S

NEED
is
Want

MAKE your way   LET GO   "THERE ARE PLACES IN THE HEART t.
NOT YET EXIST. PAIN MUST BE IN ORD
tHAT THEY BE."
- Leon Bloy

growing PAINS

t as TIME bone 8y. proof of time PASSED + Growing

BALancE   MUCK   UNSPEAKAbles

LenORD COHEN is playing. I am HOLDING
my TEARS Back with my TEETH. THis MORNing
WAS the FIRST Day 06 NEEDING my HEATER ON.

we BRokE up.

all tHIS Happened before 4 pm.

7:30 let go of alex my love

9 am chokeD on tEA

10:25 got lockED out
and HAD to CLIMB through
A TINY WINDOW
with spider WEBS

2:45 FELL
H.ARD, while
running to Buy
FILM For cAMERA

3:00 SCRAPED
a knee
b elBOW
c. SHOULDER
d. EAR

3:00 TAUGHt twO
ART and Discovery
dasses FOR the first tIME

empty SPACE

so I guess IF I could make it
through tHAT it WILL BE
OKAY.

Its that feeling of absolute
naked running
EuphoriA
through

And then
IT HITS
The unfillable
B-yearold stuck
at

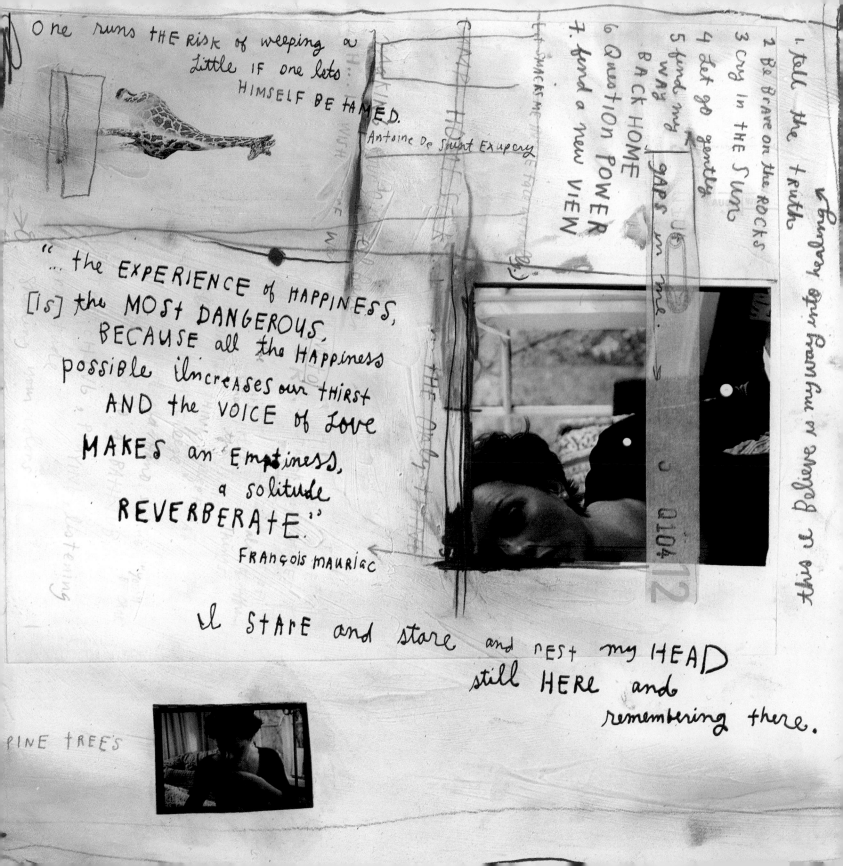

One runs THE RISK of weeping a Little if one lets HIMSELF BE TAMED.

Antoine De Saint Exupery

1. Fall the truth
2 Be Brave on the ROCKS
3 Cry in the Sun
4 Let go gently
5 find my way BACK HOME
6 Question POWER
7 find a new VIEW

GAPS in me.

"... the EXPERIENCE of HAPPINESS, [is] the MOST DANGEROUS, BECAUSE all the Happiness possible increases our thirst AND the VOICE of Love MAKES an Emptiness, a solitude REVERBERATE."

FRANÇOIS MAURIAC

I STARE and stare and rest my HEAD still HERE and remembering there.

PINE TREES

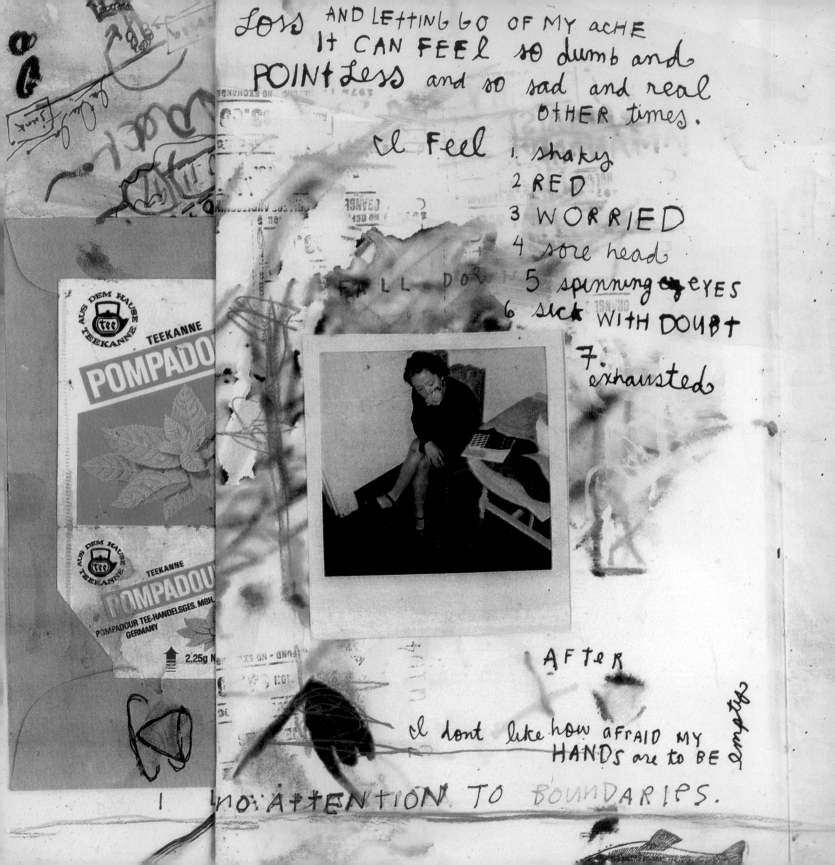

LOSS AND LETTING GO OF MY ache
It CAN FEEL so dumb and
POINTLESS and so sad and real
OTHER times.

I Feel 1. shaky
2 RED
3 WORRIED
4 sore head
FALL DOWN 5 spinning eyes
6 sick WITH DOUBT
7. exhausted

POMPADOUR

TEEKANNE
POMPADOUR

POMPADOUR TEE-HANDELSGES. MBH.
GERMANY

2,25g N

AFTER

I dont like how afraid MY
HANDS are to BE empty

1 no: ATTENTION TO BOUNDARIES.

I CAME HOME TODAY FROM SCHOOL VENTING
very Loudly IN THE CAR to MYSELF. STAGES
I FEEL SO "HIGHLY SENSITIVE" and OF
SPUNOUT and TIRED and HOPELESS Light
AND THAT FEELS SCARY! I AM TIRED
Of THIS DRAMA WITH this BOY at SCHOOL.
I WANT SINCERITY and I WANT BRAVE LOVING
I dont WANT to BE MAKING
a LOGO OR DESIGNING an Annual rePORT

I WANT TO MAKE BOOKS
AND TAKE Pictures and drink more tea
AND LIE on more couches
and Listen to PABLO NERUDA poetry
and READ SARK BOOKS
AND GO TO BED early
and KISS MORE cheeks AND
play "HEADS·up·7 up when It rains
and giggle MORE and DRIVE LESS
P AND Dream up Funny POSSIBILITIES
AND BRAVE ENDINGS.

1

2

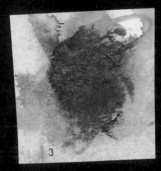

3

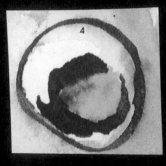

4

5

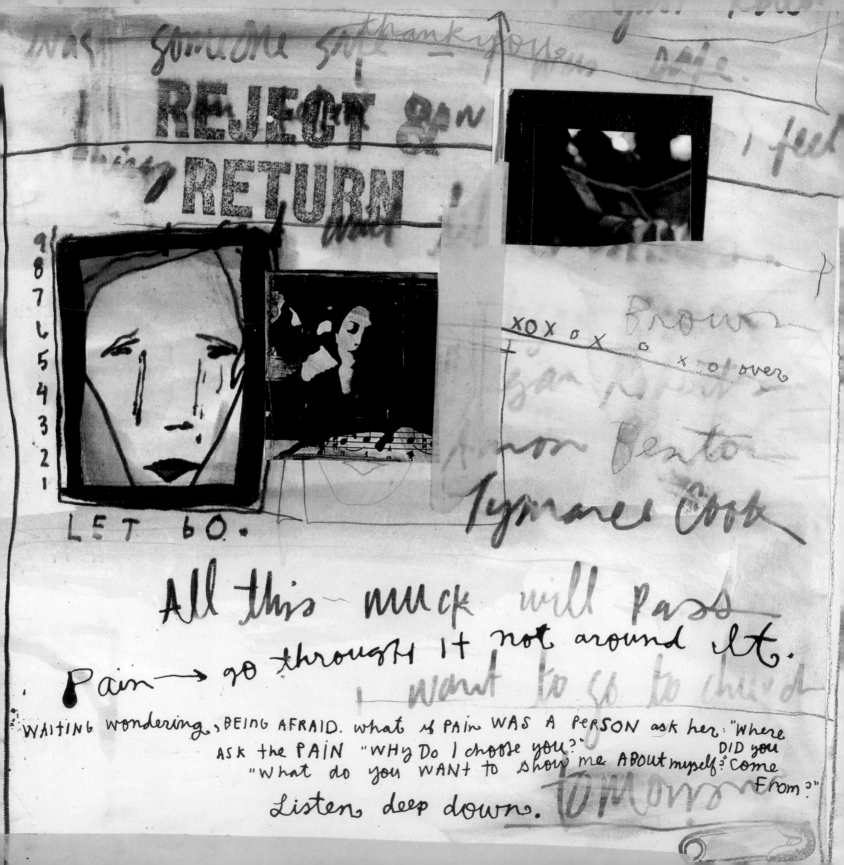

REJECT &
RETURN

LET GO.

XOXOXOoover

All this muck will pass
Pain → go through it not around it.
I want to go to child

WAITING wondering, BEING AFRAID. what if PAIN WAS A PERSON ask her "where
ASK the PAIN "WHY Do I choose you?" DID YOU
"what do you WANT to show me ABOUT myself? come
From?"
Listen deep down.

人類真是可佩

the Body is a fragile thing, but the

生命如此脆弱

一甘情願

heart can hold onto

對人

something, forever.

託付終身

A STORM HIT YESTERDAY
the moon was so Bright
that It wouldn't let me sleep.
the Day HAS Felt invisible
like time couldn't
make ITSELf known

I WANT TO TWIST
away from this
Loneliness,
there seems to Be
NO PLACE
for it in
this world
around me.

Where DOES
everybody else put their
tHEIR
Sadness.

I FEEL SAD On the underside of my skin

So who am I in this crumbled rawness?
I feel like swiss cheese →
what goes in the lonely holes?

new light?

FRESH AIR?
I've been NOTICING THE ROOTS PUSHING UP THROUGH the
SIDEWALK.
I'm trying to REMEMBER
my ROOT LOVE IN my LIFE,
FROM THOSE WHO
know me deeply.
home
1. mom
2. dad
3. Anna
4. NANA
5. megan, Brian, AARON ★

"Loss made everything sharp" - May Sarton

Driving to class with him. All I could
think about WAS
THAT IT HAD been
three days
SINCE I'd touched
his FACE.
AND HE
SEEMED
So fine.

I SAID, ~~you~~ "you seem like you
to HIM, DIDN't miss
a beat."

He looked at me
and said
"SABRINA, I've missed
SO many BEATS. I've
MADE A RhytHM."

DO I know more now?
1 MY QUESTIONS
2 MY INTUITION
3 my blushing + HOPE
4 my ACHE
were All A PART OF the
EXPERIENCE
of Falling in LOVE
and IF I DID it OVER
I'd Feel IT All again—
hopefully WORRY LESS and
Surrender MORE.

CAN't Being Just AS I Am. be enough FOR *Me* ?
I don't Like doubting my 'ME-ish-ness'
because it's ALL I HAVE
AND I don't have time to keep
SeARching to Be someone else.

HIP GIRL

I WANT the Wide HIPS And the exclamations Of delight.

WHEN did I StARt
DOUBting WHO I AM ?
my FRiend MARguerite who is TEN
just can't comprehend not Being Herself.
Thats why she is SO
VIBRANtly Alive and glorious.

Study to know YourSelf AS You ReAlly ArE
I think WE HAVE A HARD tIME MAKing A Commitment WHEN
We don't know WHO WE ArE. So who am I?
It seems to Be EASIER. to think of WHO I'm not.
★ I'm not MADonna OR SUPERMAN.

I've Been

consumed WITH ALL this living
up
to something,
to "BE SOMETHING!"
"EXPRESS SOMETHING!"
we have such a longing to Be understood
and loved By THE OTHER why?

CAn't it Be Just this now?
WITHOUT ARMOR AND SHEILDS
Just myself.
my vulnerability Protects me, not my
TIGHT CONTROL.
I HOPE TO love
WITH an Open
HAND and. A

slow trusting STRIDE.

LONG PAST DUE

Place
Tea cup
Here

THE lines of my
HAND.

TRUTH IS THAT IS ALL aBout WHO WE ARE ALReADY

TWININGS
ENGLISH
BREAKFAST
TEA

I am
In the NEW little NOOK I have made
                    In my kitchen.   (an upside down wheel as a
I have made PANCAKES and IRISH cream coffee
...A COMPLETE "Just ADD WATER BreakfAst"
I HAVE WOKEN UP with ache and a Quiet empty feeling.
   I CAN HeaR BOB Dylan IN the Backround
        singing 'I want you so BAD'
I feel   Quite lost INSIDE myself,   like im looking For my trAin tracks
        as if THEY would just   FOR my LiFe.
APPEAR and SOLVE tHE GROWING   (★ Be Blessed)
questions   Questions I seem to FACE
I seem to FACE
as il meet   my reflection
my
REFLection IN
the morning.

Perhaps we write TOWARDS WHAT we
BECOME from where we AR

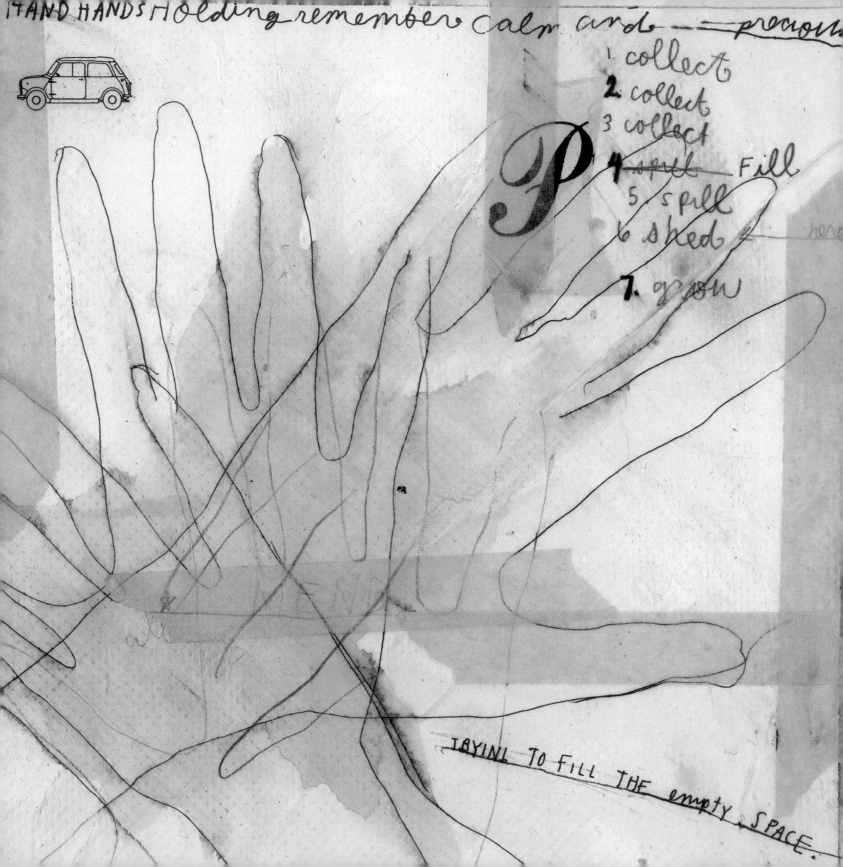

HAND HANDS Holding remember calm and ———— precious

1. collect
2. collect
3 collect
4. ~~spell~~ Fill
5. spell
6 shed
7. grow

here

TRYING TO FILL THE empty SPACE.

I don't know
    if I will
ever understand
this Ache.
    perhaps It is
Simply + completely

Love and

    what

    HAPPENS.
        at the end.

                                    ~~Loss~~ LOSS

CAN+ FIT

over

                NOVEMBER 17, early Morning

I am HERE NOW. I'm not there anymore.
with Him.
Life is carrying ON and I flash with
A MIXTURE of PANIC and faith at the truth
OF this. LIFE WILL keep GOING.

A.L GREEN is playing TIME just slips AWAY
I AM thinking ABOUT HOW MUCH I try to cling to balance
BALANCE. and the fact is
IT's not gonna feel BALANCED for a WHILE!
is REAL Living, "BALANCED" ANYWAY?

I CAN't control WHEN I HEAL. BUT I CAN WATCH
WHAT HAPPENS, and try to BE EVER-SO-GENTLE with the ACHE
WHEN im sitting
WHEN it COMES to ME ? on my floor IN A Slip
AND tEARS stuck too far down.

I FEEL a SURGE in me to Love,
and IT CAN'T BE REACHED.
I FEEL NUMB.

THERE IS A REASON
and there is A
MEANING.. you will
KNOW IN time,
BUT   time itself
                will
                    choose
        the moment
        -KENt NeRBuRN

I TALKED to NANA this morning. SHE HAS SUCH GOOD
things TO SAY ABOUt Living.
        She SAID I SHOULD TAKE CARE of the PAIN
I'm feeling. the SAME WAY I should take care of
        the scrap on MY knee, (from my Fall last week.)
SHE SAID GIVE it AIR AND SUN
        DON't PICK At IT

                Let it HEAL
So I shall immitate my knee.
        THE SCAR ON MY knee will BECOME PARt of
        A memory of the feelings of Falling on THE Ground— MY StORY.
                → AND FALLING IN LOVE.

I've Been home for a bit of family
and caring
and now my COURAGE today is to fly Home to Berkeley
even WHEN IT FEELS SO COMPLICATED
confusing and
Lonely sometimes.

"MOST OF LIFE IS JUST ABOUT SHOWING UP."
-WOODY Allen

stuff to tHINK about
and go back to
Berkeley:

1. Berry Pie
2 Hills
3 THANKSGIVING
at Amandas
☐ changing room?
Breathe
Reach Out
Swing Dancing

turning 22.

Making YOUR Life. FEEL Better.

U think it TAKES A Bit of A Lot of things.

1. let the tears roll where they will.

2. money on ANYTHING. SARK in Anyshare.

3 a VERY SOFt OLD HAND saying "you'll Be OKAY."

4. AN INVITATION to A BATHTUB.

5 stretching ————————➤ praying

6 Listening to children explain.

7. WATching the BrANCHES let GO.

8 GRATITUDE gratitude

9 sharing your colors.

forgive me.

P

lost wings

beyond

to another

1937

these are the days that's must happen to you.
— WHITMAN

this was the first time

slay

I'LL ALWAYS HOLD THIS PLACE

the C.S. Lewis love story

WELCOME

ieve

abrina

in a frame

may

So when I just feel the loss
and the sadness ———— I think,
Why love if it HURTS THIS MUCH

I try just a Bit to SOAK IN the goodness
OF FEELING

So deeply for
ANOTHER — THE
SURRENDER,
the joy; and
THE TANGLED
laughter
is also
IN the
PAIN
FELT.

"The Pain now is a
part of the happiness
then, thats the deal."
SHADOWLANDS.

the parts
selves

I have learned that trying again is important, and   decisivness is good.

I have learned that silence hurts.

I have learned about starting over

and releasing pride.

look
i

Love
RS

I have learned that frustration is allowed and talking it through
is necessary.

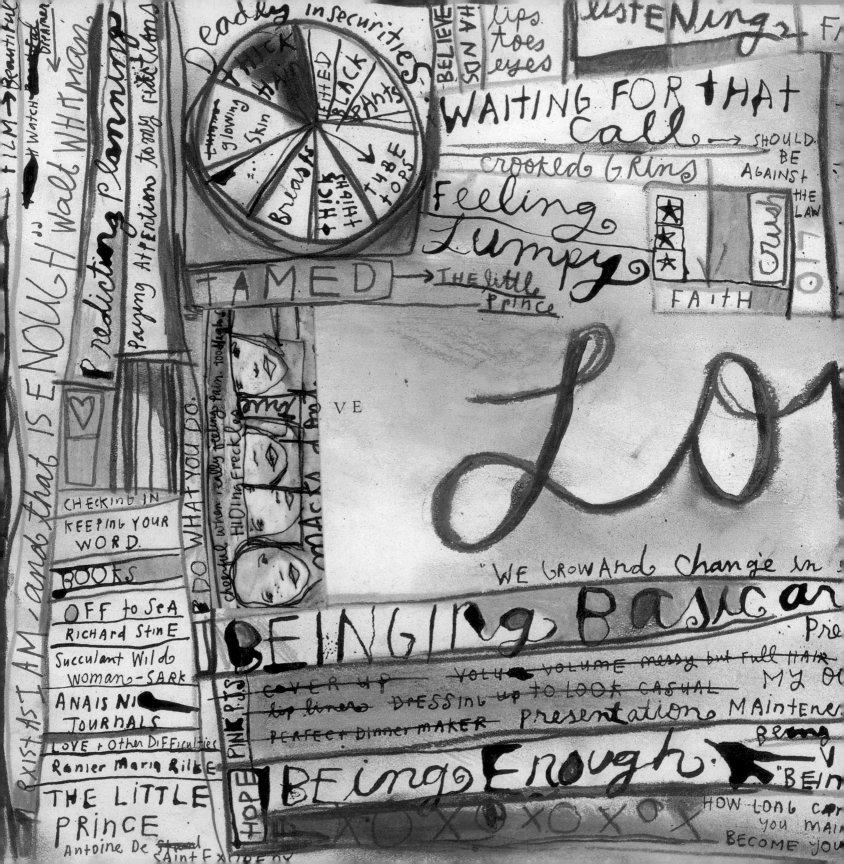

Let yourself go.

<del>from</del>

SHIFT

i just had a brainstorm of fun
things to do!
• paint your nails w/ glitter nail polish
  (i have glitter polish on my hand)
• eat Welch's lemonade popsicles
• buy pillsbury sugar cookie dough & snack heartily
• daydream about dashing   Sabrina!
  men, italian gardens, long   509
  moon lit walks   La
  don't smile like that!
remember: everything is
as it should be (seize the
uncertainty!) rest + recover FULLY before jumping
back in to it—better to be ██████ fully Sabrina again...
rather than still-sick-sleepy-achy Sabrina. You are
               magical! save my strength

BOSTON COLLEGE
Founded 1863

Harry S.Truman
USA 20c

POST CARD

From Megan.

M

Begin here

I don't want to
edit my Living,

my Becoming WHO I AM

its like trying to fit into shoes that arnt Mine   ballet slippers +
                                                    knotted RIBBons.

I've Been FEELing Blocked and FAR TOO ALONE inside,

All this Holding Back ———→ clutching on

All THE SILENT Thinking "Will he's disappear?" "How long will it last?"
                                        "K is this RIGHT?"

Maybe Im just such a Romantic, <del>this</del> wanting. treasured moments

Dreams and plans + Visions of Trips into the redwoods
Picnics on my Floor with Paint on our Fingers kisses
     FAR too much TeA and reading outloud.

sss
s   eeeeee

I just don't want the time to be spent ~~~~ wondering if it would be "TOO MUCH" to call and check-in and have a little so sweet time

Lying ── under the Oak trees At Craigmont Park

Nicola said to me this wonderful thing

" I Believe that Loving Fearlessly is the Bravest thing in this world. Its ~not~ loving without Fear. Its Loving FEAR-LESS-ly, courageously [LOVE Truly] to Be ~afraid~ afraid and leap regardless... There is such power in that. "

Let yourself go

I think that realates to all parts of living your life.

I think what is left un-lived + unexpressed in Love, Hurts the most.

NORTH BEACH PIZZA a tuesday in November with A ♡
WE ATE pizza in dim red light
We WANTED Answers and ~~so that~~
speaking into THE HARD PARTS to say.   EACH OTHERS HANDS.

it SEEMED to be
Raining Questions
and ache.

all this Fear of Love~~ing~~ your colors. and   I gave Him THE LITTLE PRINCE
makes me think of the children in
· my ART + Discovery Class. ARIEL says "I'm AFRAID of nothing
then Lilli and katie respond the SAME.
FIVE yearolds are ~~FEARL~~
FEARLESS.

(some of)
My 21 yearold Fears   the ~~the~~ NEXT class of ~~them~~ nine year olds
1. dark streets   understand WARS and burns,
2. The BACK of my Thighs,   BEing LEFt all alone + Forgotten
3 Being Laughed at   the FeAR is growing
4 Being FOllOWED   in THE
5. Being A Wimp.   DARK.
6 "JUST Being 'Lucky'   How CAN THIS HAPPEN?
7 the rain not stopping   But it keeps GOING and GOING GOOD.
8 NOT Having anything to Give.   sometimes it
9 GOSSip   feels so hard.
10. Perms   LOVE   to be brave on THE ROCKS
11. JR. High
12 ACNE   [FEAR]
13 earthquakes on Bridges   1 Recieving
14. Falling in Love   2 Replacing
15 LOVE Quitting On me   3 Re thinking
~~16.~~ 16. Dyeng ——→ worse, not really living!   4 Remembering
    5 Regreting
    6 Rejecting

It's amazing what happens when I release THE GRIP.

LOVE Love

Love today

1. Honey on crackers.

INTIMACY.

2. MY DADS VOICE
READING A STORY.

9. Unseen Laughter

delight

diet Coke and a walk around the corner.
DOOR Closing.
releasing the "whats next" worry. 6. Spilling Kisses
7 ADMitting LOVE.
Bare feet long grass. Not Feeling guilty. TEACH ME
singing loud. 8. releasing the grip. LOVE
TOASTED BAGLES

Natalie Merchant
Rosemarry Boquets 10. Singing anything
strength

TO BE MYSELF. I DON'T KNOW WHO is
I GET TIRED. FROM THE FIGURING IT ALL OUT

Before my 22nd Birthday, I would wish to commit to grow younger, to let go of my fear as I LEARN About Love. to allow All to be felt

secret answers

BELIEVE

unfold

THERE IS STILL SO MUCH Newness AND wonder to Feel

Bless tHE NOT KNOWING

I think about

★ telling my truth in Love is like exposing the underside of my wings

His o grin lines

HOW

It really feels.

right HAIR the same

HIS FINGERS SLIPED IN MINE

WE SEE THAT PART Only when we fly.

the

Only SHOULDERS

way to grow I only human connection

[DARE]

HIS that

TRUTH.

I thought a lot today about Limitless Love.
Most of the time I spend worrying
ABOUT the people in my life WHO
love me conditionally — WITH LIMITS

deciding WHEN and HOW
they will love me and
HOW they will Edit the
love they will
Show me.

The Problem lies in how I then
Edit and Limit the LOVE
I AM showing and giving
(for fear of not being loved in return)
And thats not how I want
to live in Love.

ACCOR

I sat on the bench outside of class today,
and talked to Jon.
I read to him from my journal,
it was the part about the accordian player I
was watching on the street last weekend.

He said that an accordian is such
a perfect metaphor for love,
Because you are ~~also~~
Always opening,
And closing, shifting, I saw my
And getting air, reflection
AND in the
thats Window
HOW and saw
the something
music Diffent in
happens. my eye

ARE THEY
old song's
something hard
to describe
New
ONES. true.

Muted and Tire
and rather
concerned.

the parked car
windows —
where was
she at
Twenty one?

into her pockets

☆ IF Rebecca WAS HERE I would
tell her that the pink jasmine is blooming
AgAiN.
I WOULD tEll HER THAT I
FElt AFRAiD to Ride my biKE
HOME FROM DANiels House
Last Night & ~~don~~ didnt tell
him.
I WANTED to Be embRACED
And smooched + tickled and
WONderfully whispered to
By Him but I WASNt.
I HELD BACK
I couldnt Relax

It WAS tHAt kind of holding back
tHAt I dont even know WHAt I'm
WITHOLDing—And I just ~~dso~~
Didn't know why I Felt so crumbly

missing Rebecca downstairs

TIME boes BY ~~~~~~~~~~~~~~~~~~~

spring

At Home

1	2	3
4	5
6	7	8

all in here

I Pretended to Be asleep
so I wouldnt HAVe to
deal with that awkward silence.

silence

IM just Not sure
WHAt is Going on inside
me.

WHAt Answers AM I
suppose to be arriving At?

Why AM I heRE

And
Not tHEre?

1 2 3 4 5 6 7 8 9 10

I HATE WAITing FOR A BOY

to ARRIVE!
So I wont, I'll writE. Went (or call)

I'm trying to not think ABout it →
But its so Annoying when they dont
keep their WORD!

I catch myself trying to Be cool + dont care.

The thing thAt I've been noticing
About myself is that I dont make
It clear what is important to me—
Because I dont want to
Lose the connection or seem
Like I'm too much WORK to them.

But then I Become too much WORK
FOR myself because
I'm not being True to myself.

swim

It isnt my job to judge
what is "TOO MUCH" For them
My JOB is to Be compleatly HONest and myself
and And let the other person respond honestly
With who They are and what feels right
to them.
I must not shift, ALTER or HIDE myself
IN ORDER to Experience LOVE — because
thats when thats not really Love — thAts when
resentment is BORN.

♡ OH this is what I need in Love: 1 2 3

spinning IN THE SUN and LAUGHing really silly Hard.

I need desire AND "AHHH's" and secret things and I

I need to Be told BRAVE TRUE WORDS.

yes I NEED myself just I NEED my VOICE

I need a partner who will giggle + cherish

ME to my Bones. I NEED REAL, real real

GENUiness and I need strength. I need

true. loving gestures + lots of drawing on the

FLOOR. I Need HOnest dinner time talking

I Need to Be met HALFWay. I need

to feel needed I need to Surrender surrender

I need to feel understood I need to

not Be mocked when I am Being real

I need true kindness and LOVE that

☀ ☀ ☀ GLOWS BRIGHtly

this weekend HAS felt so out of control

LOts of ~~#~~ FEARS

* Not Good at Loving

Im Not GOOD looking..

i'm NOT GOOD At Making Stuff Happen.

Im NOT GOOD At ARticULATing HOW I Feel.

...Not good at spelling

..Not good at taking care of what I love.

→ And with all these ~~----~~
Feelings comes Hopelessness

I feel like IM drowning
IN ~~to~~ feeling sorry for myself

trying to
MEASURE up

I Feel PATHetic + tireD of Being me.

sitting in THE CAR WITH Alex IN tHE Middle OF trying to get out OF tHE DARK tHICK feelings, I said "I guess it _will Be okay_"

AND HE SAID "_YES, but Its okay Now too._"

tHIs reAlly confused me because all day 1 Was trying to "GEt OVER IT."

thoughts

FORGEt my feelings
HIDE My FEElings
from HIM + From myself

I slowly began to see how right he was.

Its Okay NOW

these feelings ArE NORMAL
and have to be allowed,
→ to BE Felt and seen. ~~they are normal~~

WE HAVE to TRUSt tHAt OUR FRIENDs
WOnt Quit on us WHEN we Are HOpeless —
and even more — WE _Cant_
Quit On Our OWN selves

WE ArE all WE HAVE
deep down — and all we can save.

as i am

Ideals
Ideal
IDEAL
IDEAL
vision
OF perfect coverab

* I WANT to show
THE P.J.s before
THE BallGOWN. WHY do i WAIT
to SHOW my BASIC self, (AS IF ITS SOME SHAMEful reality)
ISN'T It MORE SHAMEFUl
loving just AS I AM.

CINCO DE MAYO
USA 32

PRIDE HIDE

make face simpleme

I WANT to stop sucking IN
$TOP Holding My Breath
STOP COVERING UP.

Let go → It isnt worth it.
I cAnt tHINK OF ONE GOOD Reason
to keep up the Act of 'Being MORE than I need
(or Less)
IF I CAN'T LOVE myself BARE + Freckled,
THEN 'HE' certainly cAnt love me.

trying to change myself to Fit Some Ideal"
SEEMS to Be An endless + DEHydrating
WAY to Live

→ fEAR of Rejection

stop

" Im AFRAID to show YOU WHO I really AM, Because if I SHOW YOU WHO I really AM, you might not Like it and thats all ive got. "

LL THE PARTS

HIDE your real Self.

HIDE YOUR ECKLES.

HEARD CE WitHOut eckles is like ky WitHOut Stars."

is just too short.

stop

Be † HIDing wHat I AM.

WHEN I WAS 11 I WAS told by A Friend in the neighborhood that A mixturE OF Lemon Juice and cottage cheese would take off my Freckles... I remember putting it all over my Arms and WAiting. I WAS HATED myself For my Freckles and thinking it would actually Work! JUst WASN't A Blonde tAN BABE. And still Am Not.

IF WE LET (les) ourselves Be TRUE truly SEEN, tHAN WE CAN BE Truly LOVED. SARK.

SLAM

★ sometimes I feel like IM in A very unloveD BODY.

dont Quit on mySelf. Its All IVE GOT.

you are so young ; you stand Before Beginning s. I would Like to Beg of you dear FRIEND as well as I can to Have PATIENCE WiTH everything that remains unsolved in your HEART. Try to LOVE the QuESTioNS themselves Like locked rooms

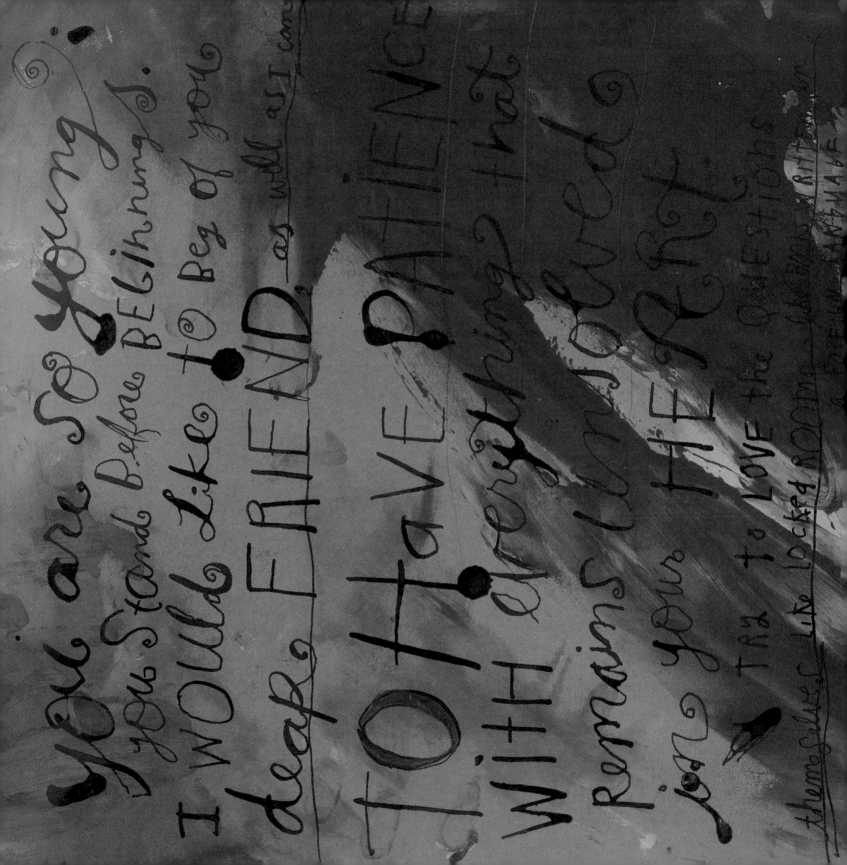

Do not now seek the answers, which cannot be given you because you could not live them. And the point is, to live everything. Live the Questions now. Perhaps you will then gradually, without even noticing it, live along some distant Day into the Answer.

— Rainer Maria Rilke

Let yourself go.

I WANT the Love in my,
Life to FEEL like A deep
BREATH, a blushing laugh,
A view across the
Sea of Cortez
ALWAYS EXPANDING and
WIDER
glowing.

I WANT the experience of love
to LIFT ME UP and
Dance during
dinner,
even when my little
SISTER says she'll
pay me $5.00 not
too.

spill open.

swing dancing
and
STAR
GAZING.

OR   PERHAPS

tell How it really feels inside.

(Loving in my own WAY.)

I AM LEARNING to reinvent WHAT being WITH A BOY CAN be like
MayBE ITS A FORT instead Of A MOVIE, WITH lots of SHEL Silverstien
reADING out loud (tHE Missing Piece meets the Big 'O' is A FAVORITe) Or A SPRING
night WITH Tea and ART On the floor.

NUT   bANANA

MOSS ROCKS
(or tacos)
(OR TACOS)
(AT TIMES)

acorns,
wheat,
black berrys,
PINE TREES
SHADOWS

AGE
LIFE
TWILIGHT +
tank top
MORNING

english
Breakfast
TEA
with
cream

NIGHT

Feeling
tHE
fabric
of the
moment
(susan talked
about this)

One day this week I found myself looking at
...great legs lined up on my

whirling
parade of jar

in LOVE

summer.

i got a tiny RED pair of
WOODEN SHOES

that

they

SAND SHADOWS

LAKE DRIBBLES
&
ideas

(I must)

Be Sure to Be ~~Be Su~~

this , (before looking ~~hard~~ for it in someone else)
(or expecting)

Today i noticed

WIDE NIGHT SKY

. BELIEVE + SUPPORT → not JoKE + MOCK
. Spills OPEN   also longined for a
                     100% silk
AKES MOONLIGHT EXplores   nighty

Wide Laughter
Loves DEEPly
tells how it Feels inside
Appreciates decadance in creative ways.
Reading Pablo Neruda in the trees shade
A tender + genuine Lover
Believing in GOD Forgiveness + wonder

faith

noon watching

MATING DRAGON FLIES

crackling FiRE... oh the smell...

OPERA MUSIC Puccini La Bohème

~~SEEING the PAIN of waiting~~
an abandoned DAD

A LAKE under a pink twilight
LOOKING LiKE Flickering SAMON

KITCH CANADA

Being enough.

susan cal
up here at
DE Gr
we laughed
laughed
spoke ge
about silen
rejection
MEN o
come for
On the
with

LOVE

Ti...

2 | thank you mom and Dad 3

the trip became an adventure of sorts

MOM + DADs anniversary is Today

CANADA

a goodnight + goodbye

20 years of hanging Out together

THE NORTH STAR
horse shows
Reflection On the NAVY lake

• tHE Sound of EARly morning coffee + Ideas

De brassi

whistle of cricketo
garden talking
Crackle FIRE

HAVing children

PAD tHAi
NIGHt HUM

Laughing HARD

H.O

Italian dinners
an Old pal to
notes

cooking Wild Dinners

Being Real Deep supporters

the dock

COMPANIONS

Pals

secret trail

Lovers

PARents

i wonder if i will ever know
this feeling One day?
(i really hope so. reALly. REALLY.)

A Weekend in San Diego with
dear Brian

my Best Boy(Friend)Brother wish:
A
picnic over the Ocean at
                        sundown
with laughter + wide
                    conversations
all I could wish for

perspective

picnic

years

Brians Friendship
Arrived some summer,
afternoon years ago,
with Bare Feet,
and a grim.

Brian

HE IS a FRIEND WHO asks
DEEP Life Questions, LISTENS passionately
And tickles greatly

HE teaches me
to live it all
the doubt — THE DESIRE
the OVERWELMING ache,
Because you feel so deeply
is good — it is real

HE reminds me that
"the QUEST is to BECOME all
that you already ARE."

I FEEL much better after our ocean walk, we
talked about GOD's Huge love and acceptance of us AS IS, hard to

I WANT to TOUCH ON All THE Sides
OF LOVE — THE HOPE + Gladness
as WELL as THE ANXIETY + Ache.

THE BIGGest thing About Love that
I HAVE DISCOVERED IS thA LOVE Isn't.
JUST ONE WAY — there isn't just
A Point of PERFECTION THAT MAKES
it "All okay + bread FROM NOW ON."

I am discovering thAt what I
am needing to learn in love is gonna
KEEP coming up. Oh yes!
    THIS MORNING I WOKE UP From A VERY restless
sleep with Anxiety about replacement
And I just exclaimed to myself

HAVEN'T I LEARNED this YEt?!

haven't I learned HOW to handle these
    Feelings yet? the answer: NOPE.

"FOR ONE human being to LOVE another is perhaps the most difficult task of all, the epitome, the ultimate test. It is that striving FOR which ALL OTHER striving is merely PREPARATION."
RAINER MARIA RILKE

MOM MY AGE + TRUER

I AM learning to write + speak OF MY tRUE Feelings for myself. THATS HOW I CAN Let Go sooner + LOVE Fuller. It's [A] MIXTURE OF speaking up + speaking in. reaching out and

rEACHing IN.

Pine wood the World.
DANGLING Bits of the world.

← Alexander S

t H is way.

lemon HONEY Drink
SHORt HAIRe + GINGER tEA
ROME

OH whAt AM I learning? ...sKETCHbooks
smell d.ffrent
From One anotHER.
to Be alive — to Be Okay WITH all thAt
I Don't understAnd still. (driving to SANtA Pauls
just to get to tHE
All tHE "HOW COMES" and BOY I wAnt to kiss.)
"MayBe I shoulds"

Tonight, Alex and I SAt in A dim Booth sipping COkES,
I knew again Why all of tHis—
To grow — more alive.
to experience being alive and being Brought alive
by another
somEthing & so beautiful and rare.
it reminds me of that Henry Miller
line...
a. laughing
B. PAPER
a. crying
D. listening new
e. photos view SKY "I want to become more +
F. TIME more myself as ridiculous as thAt
G. music MAY sound."
H. cArs
I. SeA
J. Books in LOVE I Become WHO I MUSt understAnd.
K. BeDs
L. kissing i miss you

I FIND MYSELF

COMPARING a Lot — thinking "OH I SHOULD be MorE
LikE her" "he is less LikE HIM" La La La.
But when I let go of the world all
around me and BreAtHE into ME as I AM — I can
LOVE much more truly + compleatly — ~~too~~
WHEN I can accept myself I can accept the ones
around me.

And BE still
together
enough as WE are.
that the real PArt.
(connect)
all THERE is.

all THERE IS
all THERE is.
REAL IS all THere is.

MOM + DAD

Sometimes I serge with power.
Sometimes I am unable to buckle down my euphoria.
Sometimes I feel really terrable.
Sometimes I want to go home.
Sometimes I hate my body.
sometimes I want someone to love all   my faults.
Sometimes I don't want anyone to look at me.

Sometimes I don't say what I feel.
Sometimes I v regret what I did. .
Sometimes

sometimes wish I was six.

Sabrina Ward Harrison

It is now noon ✶ roma cafe ✶

IVE GOT THIS GREAT NEW PEN.
to write with, this afternoon
AND THAT SEEMS to BE the
only thing, that is getting me
TO WRITE SOMETHING

I HAVE Been coloring-in
previous BARE PAGES

and drinking + redrinking my
CUP OF JASMINE tEA.

A ive HAD three cups of tea.
B three PITA BReAD some hummus
C and A non-FAt YOGERT ← yogert # is a
                              HARD WORD to
                              spell

also read ←
BIRD
BY
BIrd.

I HAVE Been WATCHING A
WOMAN A FEW tABLES AWAY
reading ANNE Lamott
HEr BOOK operating instructions
so many expressions
covered her FACE as SHE reads from pale to page.
THAt BOOK Brought me so
much Laughter and
Quiet thinking. BOOKS like
tHAt ARE Such Blessings
tRUtHFUL_BRAVE_RARE .
I keep thinking ABOUt
WHEN I will Begin my
BOOK" AND that overwhelms me
Compleately...THE tRUth is it has
Been written inside me and
IN tHE RIGHt TIME MY BOOK WILL EMERGE to the World

I AM WATCHING THE CARS BUSES, CABLE CARS and PEOPLE — ALL going UP and DOWN, EVERYONE IS on their way to A DESTINATION somewhere. BUT it seems like THE "JOURNEY THERE" is REALLY where the secret DETAILS ARE the things WE ARE to be learning — THE corners AND EDGES OF OUR STORIES. Every MOMENT 'ON THE WAY' is the destination.

READ: MOONLIGHT CHRONICLES

It feels hard to write.
I just don't want to.

                    but it's only the second day of this
                         new "MORNING WRITING " goal,
          I didn't sleep well last   night.
                    (I got the couch) it was really deep
                                        and i felt like
                         I was sinking, *all night*
          I got all twisted up and now my back hurts, it was really windy
          and the shutters were banging.
                    and the worst part is that yesterday I tripped really badly.

TODAY

I FEEL 15.
     and...
                    while running down the pathway to the beach with my sister
                         (she will make me admit that I was sort

1. dry
2. thick   of going after a very cute boy
3 chapped   ) anyway...
                    I went flailing into the air ~~with~~ my high sandles
4. Lumpy   (*yes*)
                         I banged up the ball of my foot and
5. Beige   now it's blue and hurts.
                         ~~now I don't want to write.~~
Six. WIDE
                    how is that for complaining?
7. Freckled   oh yes, and I also have ~~aloe~~ vera in my eye.
   (extra)   *ALOE*
                    this sounds like Alexander and the Terrible Horrible
                    no good ↓day   by Judith Viorst
                              ↓ VERY BAD.
SOME DAYS ARE LIKE THIS.   and its's only 9am.

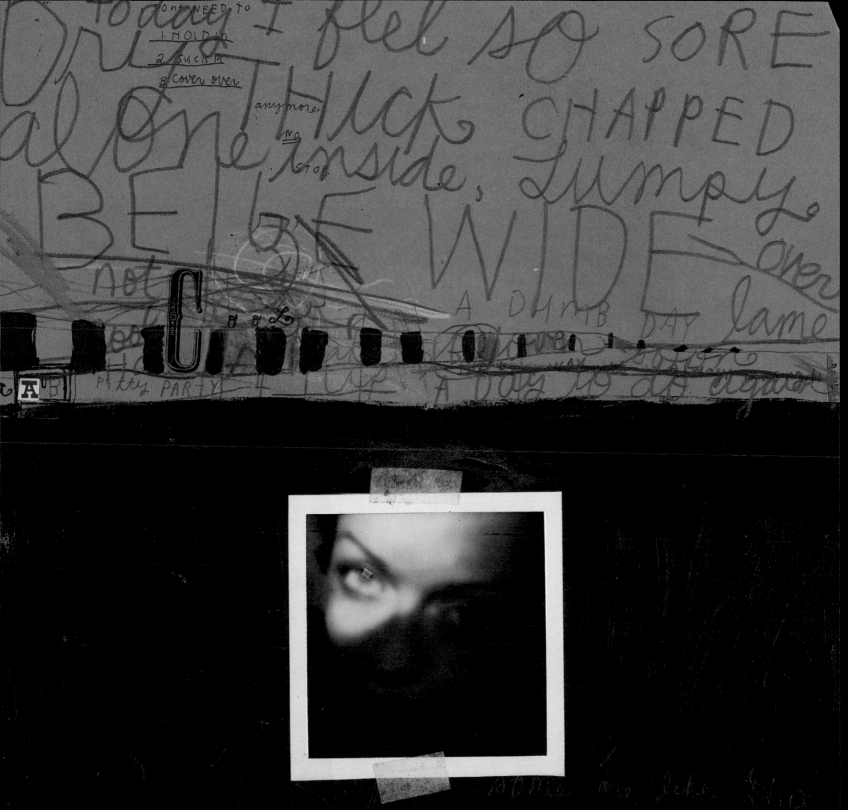

compare compare compare compare compar

$

I just CAME HOME FROM a day At the MALL.
WHAT was I thinking? THE with myself.
I THINK I WENT— to get Away FROM my thinking.

ROAMING WITH PLATFORM BOOts
AND BLACK- suckin tummy PANts...
I was DRESSED TO BLEND INTO the mall.

my FEET ACHE   I'VE Been
                      search SEARCHING outward
                              not inward.
And I'VE GOt Red rubbed marks on my   I feel TIRED.
                      Anckles
GOOD?   SORE   WHERE THE ZIPPER
Legs.   on my too HIGH BOOts
                      WEre scratching my Legs as I
measuring myself
1   2   3   4   5   6   7 8   9   climbed up
                                               and down the
                                               ESCALATORS.
                                               Looking for
                                               Outward
                                               answers.

Sometimes
Sometimes I hate my body. Sometimes I wish I was six.

school

I am

soup.

Beet
Butternut
soup

LUNCH at school.
eating lunch
I'M IN ONE OF THOSE compleatly
DISCONNECTED FROM MY BODY sort OF MOODS.
mental
I CAN TELL
that MY HAIR

is flat +
wing-y on
THE sides

I want
to relax

I really DO

Why does it matter so much here?
so MUCH WATCHING
and FEELing
WATCHED.
—trying too hard—
sometimes I go to the Bathroom to LOOK in THE
MIRROR
just
to MAKE
sure I'm still here
GET A GRIP
MY MIND CAN TAKE
ME SO FAR AWAY

awful awful awful awful

HOLDING

AM AH

finding myself alone.

I MADE A COMFORT STATION IN MY LOCKER to LOOK INTO WHEN I FEEL LOST FROM THIS WORLD.

...times I want to go home.

IT IS FILLED WITH

1. Jasmine tea
2. EARL GREY TEA (HONEY PACKETS.)
two MUGS
angel cards   Honey

SOME SNACKS
GUM
RED LICORICE
ginger candy

CHILDHOOD PICTURE
Present DAY family
picture

ANNE Lamott
lavender lotion
COMB.

SARK

Sometimes

...ust Be Brave!
(Grateful)

...ING to HOLD ONTO   I FEEL LIKE
TIME. NEW TIME

FULL

CRY

grass is greener?

REMEMBER to
READ

JOURNAL
OF A solitude
BY May Sarton
and

PABLO NERUDA
(THE BOOK of Questions)

...HOUT COLOR   I try too much to Protect + HOLD WHAT I WANT ON to... BE FREE

...eyes.

JENNY READ by Jenny Read

my whole body was overcome with the ache of inadequac

You are what you believe.

TODAY we were sitting watching a video ON MTV and he said "oh she is ALL WOMAN" my whole body was overcome with the ache of inadequacy

my inner VOICE IM NOT ENOUGH I said I AM NOT ENOUGH I kept thinking silently IM not this

my body is the only thing I really can truly take care of

BETRAY MYSELF

tall breathy curvy breasty singer, WOMAn BEAUTY lalala

Don't have time for this

I should do this

grateful my BODY

I and I can't leave it I can't abandon the only thing I can truly take care of

So this is the only BODY this is the only kind of judging Oh I shouldnot be filled with this amazing adventures

NOT GOOD enough stunning enough it is me that hurts myself BECAUSE I listen to the HURTING VOICES inside ME

it was the SADDEST SELF BETRAYAL

☆☆☆☆

I HATE BEING JEALOUS OF WOMEN just sitting THERE Quietly tearing myself APART

I LEAVE my own side AGAIN

like BECky said "there will always be more beautiful WOMEN - SMARTER WOMEN - more successful women always, so you must FOCUS On WHAT YOU ARE, not WHAT you arnt.

I NEED to breathe deep breathes into myself, not sew myself shut with tight DOUBT turning against yourself is betraying what created you

IM trying to WAKE up.

IM trying to GROW
IM trying to WAIT

IM trying to UNDERSTAND.   IM trying to listen "

<u>IM TRYING TO BE BRAVE.</u>

Im trying to BELIEVE
    Im trying to HOLD ON
Im trying to SurrENDer
IM trying to 'BECOME'
    Im trying ————→ " FORGET

        Im trying to sea

here we really are,, sgive me your hand

Sometimes I feel really terrible.
Sometimes I serge with power.
Sometimes I want to go home.

The BeST Way Out is is Always through.
~R. frost

" If I had my life to live over again I'd try to make more
     mistakes next time. I would relax. I would Limber up.
I'd be sillier than I have been on this trip. I know of
a very few things I would take seriously.
     I would be less hygenic. I would take more chances
     I would take more trips.
I would climb more mountains, swim more rivers,
               and watch more sunsets.
     I would burn more gasoline and eat more ice cream
               and less beans.
I would have actual troubles & fewer imaginary ones.
     you   see I'm one of those people who lives sensibly
     and sanely hour after hour, day after day.

               oh, I've had my moments, ~~and if I had my~~
in fact I'd have nothing else ~~just moments~~ LIFE TO LIVE OVER I'd have more of them.

     just ──────→ moments one after another

          instead of living so many ~~days~~ years ahead each day.
     I've been one of those people who never goes anywhere
without a theremometer, hot water bottle, rain coat &
and parachute.

          If I had my life to live over I'd go places and do
THINGS AND TRAVEL LIGHTER THAN I have.
     ~~I would~~ If had my life to live over I would start
          Barefoot earlier in the spring & stay that way
          later in the fall. I would play hooky more.
     I wouldn't make such good grades, except by accident.
I'd ride more merry-go-rounds. I'd pick more dasies."

          NADINE STAIR   age 85

And IF I HAD my LIFE to LIVE OVER I'D HAVE MORE OF THEM. IN FACT I'd have nothing else

Live

I HAD a pretty major talk with mom tonight On the phone..

I HAVE FELT FRUSTRATED with our Friendship. KIND.

I DON'T Like Calling HOME just for the "news".

I WAnt to feel needed + connected +

~~Valuable~~ VALUABLE. LATELY it HAS Felt like AIR

Empty of the Real stuff.

I Am so Glad we could talk about it. I think

WE cracked through the shell to the

REALNESS of OUR FRIENDSHIP as Mother + DAUGHTER.

I Came FROM HER → I want to KNOW HER → ~~truly~~ TRULY.

Crimson HONEY, COMB CANDLES Tonight

grow

NARCISSUS ~~Narcissus~~ BULBS I Bought THREE

Celebrating the Self

I HOLD tightly to FRIGHTENED HANDS.
And kiss ForeHEADS gently.

WALT WHITMAN

READ song of yourself

I tellmy truth

I MAKE a lot of mistakes

I tell my doubts

I LAUGH WITH my worries

I DANCE With little girls and I

WATCH SEA TurtLes WITH NANA.

I am Frightened By TRUTH sometimes ——→ But I need it
LIKE My OWN BLOOD

I know WHAt its like TOO FEEL to deeply and wander and WONDER under the LATE DAY sun today alone

OPEN UP.

FINDING MY STYLE AND not wearing
Fitted BLACK PANTS.

IF I WAS to HAVE An ANSWER
to this Growing PAIN
Question
it would Be
Something like
THIS:
you've got
this AMAZING cREATURE ——> YOURSELF.
THAT CAN move and Breathe, DANCE and, cry.
And you have a certain amount OF MOMENTS
(MAYBE a Few million moments — But
AND YOU HAVE THIS CHANCE to do absoloutly
MOMEnts THEY ArE)
ANYTHINb
to rEACH OUT to AnotHEr vulnerable +
TRUE.
to dance on the roof in euphoriA
AND PRAY BESIDE tHE OCEAN
to LEt GO
WE HAVE THE CHANCE every MOMENT to
BE ALIVE and to GIVE to THIS
WORLb WHO nEEds EACH OnE OF
US SO BADLy

SABRINA, remember—

I don't have to be cool.

→ I do not HAVE to BE slender. I do not have to be Tricky.

I do not have to Be smooth.

no no no more

A b c d e f g h

I DO not HAVE TO Be silent.

I do not have to Be LOUD.

I DO not HAVE to Be slick

I DO not HAVE TO BE HER. I do not
I do not have to hide who I am
HAVE TO BE loved, BY HIM. to Be okay.

(I) do not HAVE to Hold on so tightly.

I do not HAVE to Agree to Be accepted
I do not have to wear covers up. I do not
have to Be covered up. I DO not HAVE to predict.
I DO not HAVE TO PREPARE (for the pain.) I do
not HAVE to GRASP. I do NOT HAVE TO
have the answer. I do not have to
Be better. I do not have to Be cool. I only
HAVE to Be WHO I am.

→ MY OWN BODY

I HAVE to take care. (HONOR)

I HAVE to DANCE in my BEDROOM + wear my own skin

YElLOW BRICK ROAD

I know HOW TO LIE DOWN and stare at the sky and wonder about this
Life of mine.

I know I love macaronni with ketchup

* I know HOW TO slide my fingers along his neck and think
about HOW much
IT will
ACHE at the end.
I KNOW I am strong + soft and sore other times
I KNOW I AM LOVED IN HUGE Deep ways.
surrender to change
I know I'm afraid.
OF tHAt to go Away.

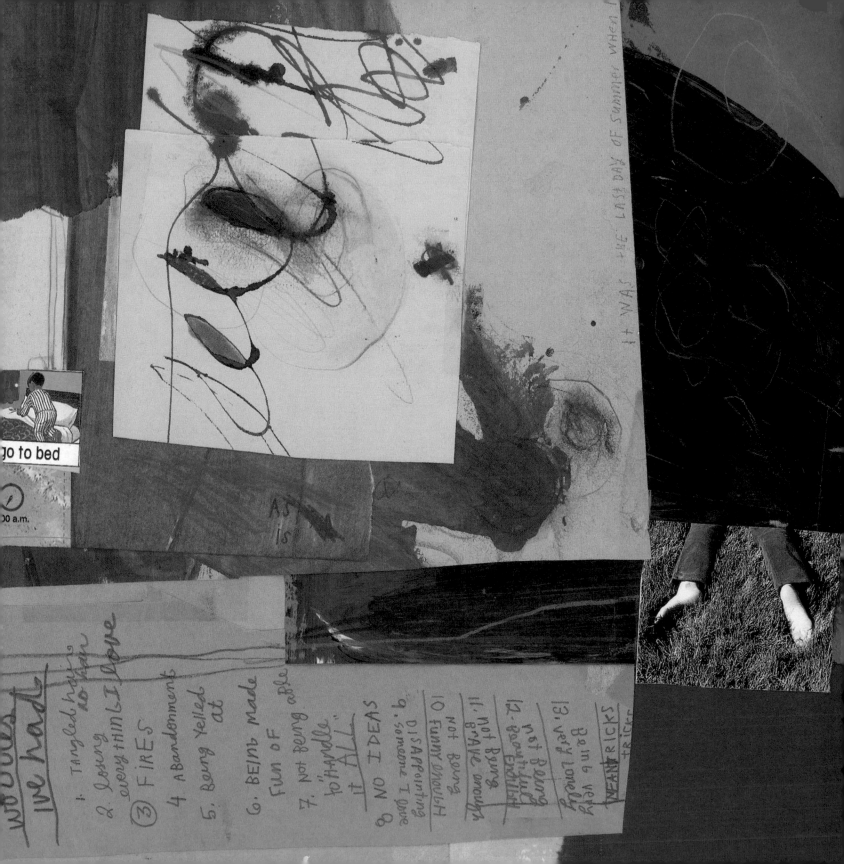

go to bed

00 a.m.

IT WAS THE LAST DAY OF SUMMER WHEN

AS
IS

WOULD we had!
1. Tangled hair to han
2. losing everything I love
③ FIRES
4. ABandonment
5. Being Yelled at
6. Being made Fun of
7. Not being able to "Handle it ALL"
8. NO IDEAS ON
9. someone I love
10. Funny enough
DISAPPOINTING
11. Not being BRAVE enough
12. Beautiful Enough
not being
13. very lonely
Being very loved

NEAT RICKS
TRICKS

I see myself rushing around MAINTAING and →PREPARING←

FOR WHAT "WILL HAPPEN Next"
and THE WORRies that go along with it
getting READY FOR LIFE—not Being IN LIFE
it seems We START SO YOUNg WITH THE

get up | dress | wash | eat | work | undress | bath

Routine.

NE "GROW up" too FAS

If we STop there ARE So many
WORRiES OF WHAT could happen
will I ~~four~~ LosE the connection?
will I BE REPLACED?
will I BE Forgotten? N

it IS EXHAUSTING - Gripping
onto too much!

I AM REMINDED OF MAY SARTon WRiting
IN JOURNAL OF A SOLITUDE

"IMMITATE THE TREES"

Let GO. cut off excess...prune
WAIT. WATCH. grow deep

WILL IT BE TAKEN AWAY?

REMEMBER 4HN DAY.

AWAY   A   WAY

ALL
WAY

these day

I tHink bOD leaves me Alone to let
ME FIND MY OWN STRENGTH
BECAUSE no ONE else can give it TO ME
FOR ME
sometimes it is very lonely - but
I know the lonely times TEACH
Me the Most.
In must let go in order to let anything in

no ONE CAN LOVE ME. FOR ME.

take a Big Walk
protected in the
trees

BEFORE
I MISS THE time Before   today

3

Bob Dylan
~~Ani DiFranco~~
Leonard Cohen
Indego Girls
★ all you need.

music.

we tumble home again.

LISTENing.

LATE SUMMER BEGINNING

we see

thank

nana

epiphanies.
alone

from LETTERS to A Young Poet BY: RAiNER MARIA RILKE

Read

Think, dear friend, reflect on the world that you carry within yourself. And name this thinking what you wish. It might be recollections of your childhood or yearning for your own future. Just be sure that you observe carefully what wells up within you and place that above everything that you notice around you. Your innermost happening is worth all your love. You must somehow work on that.

Iowa

memories

Down The Center By Canoe

me. companions Solitude FEAR Looking

...to you is a dashing and bold
adventure.

→ № 1 SHOES dancing) (SWING

2 eggs

3 plateS ITAlian Dinners in the garden

4 tops (TUBE tops + BOAt Necks)

5 teA earl grey + cream

6 bathtubs under the MOON

7 grapefruit, With honey

8 buttons c.p. theles

9. tomatos from daniel.

WATER   TEA

draw.

Make Your own life.

I've been away from Berkeley for a week. I feel like I disappeared from the world —THAT WORLD— and came home in such a larger sense of the word. Tonight we made berry pie and ~~ate~~ asparagus with our fingers (like Walt Whitman). We watched the great movie 'Beautiful Dreamers' under lots of quilts

I love this
funny family
of mine

At **home** (Last day of summer)
It is GOOD to sit HERE under
Huge knarled OAK trees in the late
AFTERNOON It feels like life
HAS slowed down→to just look up at the
sky with MY DAD

I   I feel nearly only 8

I ←

HERE I can Rest And Be AS
YOUNG AS I AM

★ TAKE this feeling WITH ME.

I FEEL THE END OF THIS BOOK
arriving.

↓

You know it is HAPPENing
when THE spine begins
and suddenly   → to creek
    the BOOK has
BECOME RIPE

WHAT a year it Has BEEN.
all these 1. QUESTIONS
           2. Miracles
           3. MUCK
           4 ClARity.
    that HAVE come from   → simply trying
                                  TO GROW
                                  into MYSELF

(I think Growing Happens even when
         —Im not trying.

ThEre HAS Been   A full room

a lot of
TAKing In
And Letting
    GO.
And GOODByes.

MEGAN
FAITH →

BElong to yourself   First PAInting ←

our Freckles

WE SPEAK even when we
are no longer
speaking.

and oh how very you

live been searching

A SHOW IDEA

I AM FINALLY HERE SITTING ALONE to
feel life - digest my
GROWING

Aunt Ann is dying and I feel
REGRET that I didn't HEAR
all HER STORIES

her time PARIS in the 20's

I WISH I HAD ASKED HER MORE Questions
tell me tell me (we should
LIFE really is so short   always
                                              ask further)
WE HAVE SUCH LITTLE TIME
With eachother   listen. Bless.

COME BACK TO ERIN

ⓐ weeping Willow Today it
ⓐ a storm of rest Aunt
ⓐ tiny wonder

@ weeping Willow
@ a storm of rest
• tiny wonder

She offered
the Old Photo
I wonder
who you will one day find
I CAN'T sl... begged Her to say goodbye.
I feel like I HEAR HER

WHY is it when we know someone   though
us → why is it then THAT WE CAN   is leaveng
love them the ↓ DeepEst?   the closest TIME
IS WHEN WE SAY   gOODBye.
BedTIME

love all the way
STORY

while I CAN

knowing someone else's
life is passing away
MAKES me want to show up For LIVING now—
not 'THEN' when
'things' are taken care of and the WEATHER IS WARM.
TODAY I have a chance to make a
diffrence NOW.
I Have a chance tO HELP heal some of my OWn BROKEN Places
and hopefully someone elses.
☆ WE MUST REALIZE THAT WHAT WE DO

Before we
knew HOW
to leave
eachother

Matters
what remains OUr love matters' truly
long after I AM gone that is gOOd for others
(THATs WHY We ARE HERE)

Life is too short to Be cruel, IT IS TOO SHORT
tO suck-in, HOLD IN, NOt FORGIVE WE JUSt DOn't
Have time
love is all there is to DO

FORGIVE YOURself

Signatures at various ages

Betty Bartman 7 yrs.
Betty Bartman 10 yrs.

Sabrina Ward Harrison

WE ARE
NOT SO different
only our
circumstances
are.

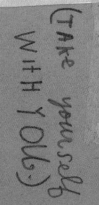

(TAKE yourself
WITH YOU.)

don't turn against YOURSELF.
bottom → top
mind
→ SOUL.

n from W

I CAN'T BE HERE JUST TO WORRY ABOUT THE ZIT on my CHIN, OR the 'sexier' Girls than me OR MY BUTT-to-THIGH transition → AND HOW much. I WANT HIM TO CALL.

I HAVE to be here to do my PART to be truly me As Bravely As POSSIBLE → WITH myself — WITH Others. I must give what I know is TRUE. for my own like I MUST Be REAL! means always reminds me "THE WORLD looks so different WHEN YOU remember to Be one of NOT image".

HOW WE ARE
MY WHOLE BODY
→ Inner voice →

So here I am

today.
In the story
of
my life.

This is what I
know now.
These are my
Questions
I ask.

mostly it's
tangled

but it's real.

and very little
seems
to be real anymore.

collect your

life.

treasure.

I am here alone for the first time in

weeks, to take up my "real" life again at last.

That is what is strange—that friends,
  even passionate love, are not my real life

unless there is time alone in which to explore

and to discover what is happening or has happened.

MAY SARTON, JOURNAL OF A SOLITUDE

1. DOnt compromise yourself
→ free → FREE → yourself

stAY on your Own shore

feel it
ALL the the way through Clear ~~the~~ night sky
the weak
the strong
the real.

LIE DOWN under a

And ~~for what~~ What LIStEN

to → WHAT Falls silent behind your gaze.

Growing up is like this. living is like this
The Euphoria and the Ache,
the Confusion and the Question.
the WONDERING, the understanding, the young and the Brave.

these Are the DAYs
THat must HAPPEN
to me. this I Believe

BE yourself BE YOURSELF

CONTRADICTIONS EMBRACE them.
Own them.
→ Laugh with them.

I am Learning that.

WE Are all of it. All of our edges
the BASIC the AngRy the lonely the brave the true the lost the SCARED

THERE isn't going to BE A point
of COMPLEATION (that is the hard part to realize)
IM not going tO 'have' it all together'

LOOK ⊙ How I "should Look"
→ feel how I "should feel" and
DO what I "should BE doing"
because right now is it Because right now is it.
I don't know WHAT will come next → How it will come
know. it neVER WORKS Out how I think it WILL
LOOKing BACK it always has do worked Out How
it SHOULD.

remember this   as we go on our own way.

What I really want to say to myself is

IT is ALRight

THIS → right Here this mess this

as my friend GAry says "IN its Own

FlaWED WaY, It is all secretly perfect

these anxious → Questions, DOUBts

answers and waiting → this is just as

it is → right NOW → taking me on my

way → don't run. We all suffer

there will be This is what I know to be

understanding

A → sooner than you think and later than you expected

sometimes Im just such A Mess.

Study? THAT voice inside that wispers **YES**

I have learned

→ more is never enough. the world waits for you.

~~We~~ Writing A BOOK is really your

HARD.

and takes a really long time.

and a hell of alot of FAITH

writing is mostly about letting GO and loosening

the muscles of the heart

I am learning that growing is a mixture

Of surrendering to that none of it matters

And All of it Matters.

The DetAils of our lives and

our truth _it is about_ → WHAT WE STAND

UP FOR → and what

WE Let gO Of. this is the ~~real stuff~~

Accepting myself brings me
AWAY FROM ANALYZING
DOUBTING comparing
ALTERING HOW I AM
WHO I AM

It GIVES ME SPACE to DANCe
and BE BAREFoot and ForGIVE and
Write brAVELY even WHEn it Feels scary and
AWKWARD, it is WHO I Am
It is important TO SHARE and
NECESSARy to live.
As "tangled and TRUE as it is.

I AM realizing that I am enough as is → a WORK IN PROGRESS

I HAVE looked at the Love that surrounds me...the new LOVE and HIDDEN LOVE, and DESIRED LOVE. BUT SOMETHING changes when I SLOWLY turn my LOVE towards myself thats when my LIFE BECOMES VIVIDLY FULL color. I think in healing ourselves WE can take Part in healing the WORLD I CAN see the Life in me, I can stop HIDING my FRECKLES I CAN Look deeply into my own eyes, And high up into tHE Branches of trees. I can BECOME myself...

" Love it all.
THE FEAR,
THE EXCITEMENT
the guilt
THE POWER FOR
CHANGE
the UNWORTHINESS
the HURT
FEELINGS
the euphoric
feelings
THE ANGER
the MOVEMENT,
the Whole process,
It's Known
as Life "
—unknown

SAbrina

MARIA

1 2 THREE 4 5 SIX 7 8 9 10

DAN MEG BRI + SA
Summer 1994

TIKA TARO

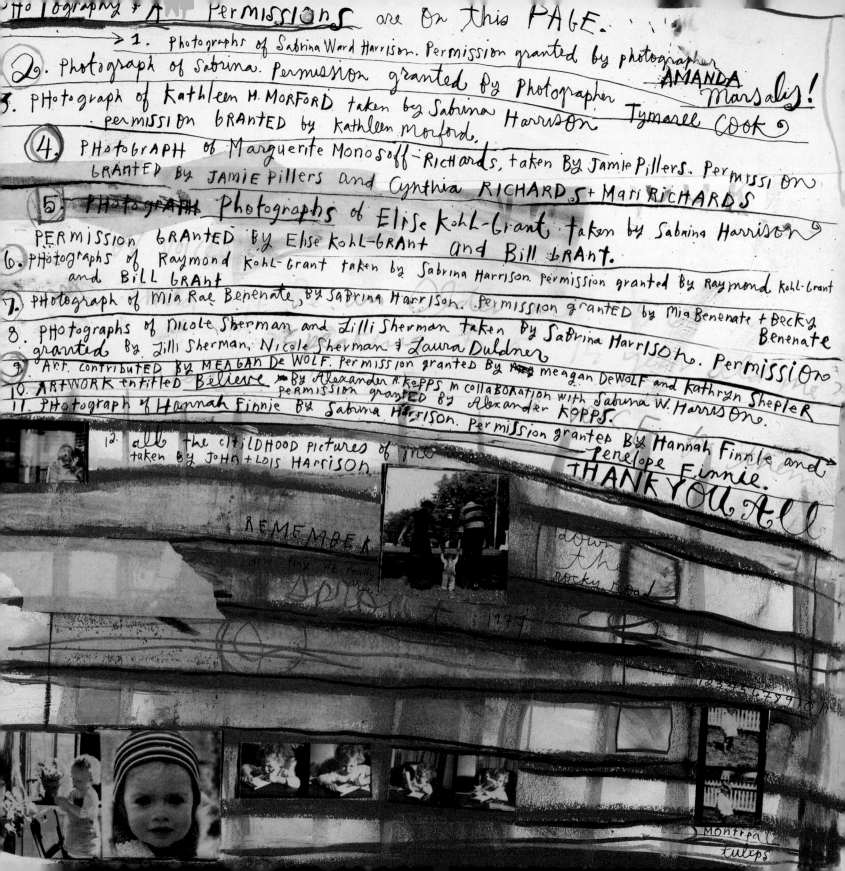

Photography + Art Permissions are on this PAGE....

→ 1. Photographs of Sabrina Ward Harrison. Permission granted by photographer

2. Photograph of Sabrina. Permission granted by Photographer AMANDA Marsalis! Tymarel Cook

3. Photograph of Kathleen M. MORFORD taken by Sabrina Harrison. permission BRANTED by Kathleen Morford.

4. PHotograph of Marguerite Monosoff-Richards, taken By Jamie Pillers. Permission GRANTED By JAMIE Pillers and Cynthia RICHARDS + Mari RICHARDS

5. PHotograph Photographs of Elise Kohl-Grant, taken by Sabrina Harrison PERMISSION GRANTED BY Elise Kohl-Grant and Bill GRAnt.

6. PHotographs of Raymond Kohl-Grant taken by Sabrina Harrison. permission granted By Raymond Kohl-Grant and Bill GRAnt

7. PHotograph of Mia Rae Benenate, By Sabrina Harrison. Permission granted by Mia Benenate + Becky Benenate

8. Photographs of Nicole Sherman and Lilli Sherman taken By Sabrina Harrison. Permission granted By Lilli Sherman, Nicole Sherman + Laura Duldner

9. Art contributed By MEAGAN De WOLF. Permission granted By meagan DeWolf and kathryn Shepler

10. ARTWORK entitled Believe By Alexander R. Kopps in collaboration with Sabrina W. Harrison. permission granted By Alexander KOPPS.

11. PHotograph of Hannah Finnie By Sabrina Harrison. Permission granted By Hannah Finnie and Penelope Finnie.

12. all the childhood pictures of me taken By JoHn + Lois Harrison

THANK YOU ALL

REMEMBER
how fine we really are...
1977
down the rocky road

Montreal tulips

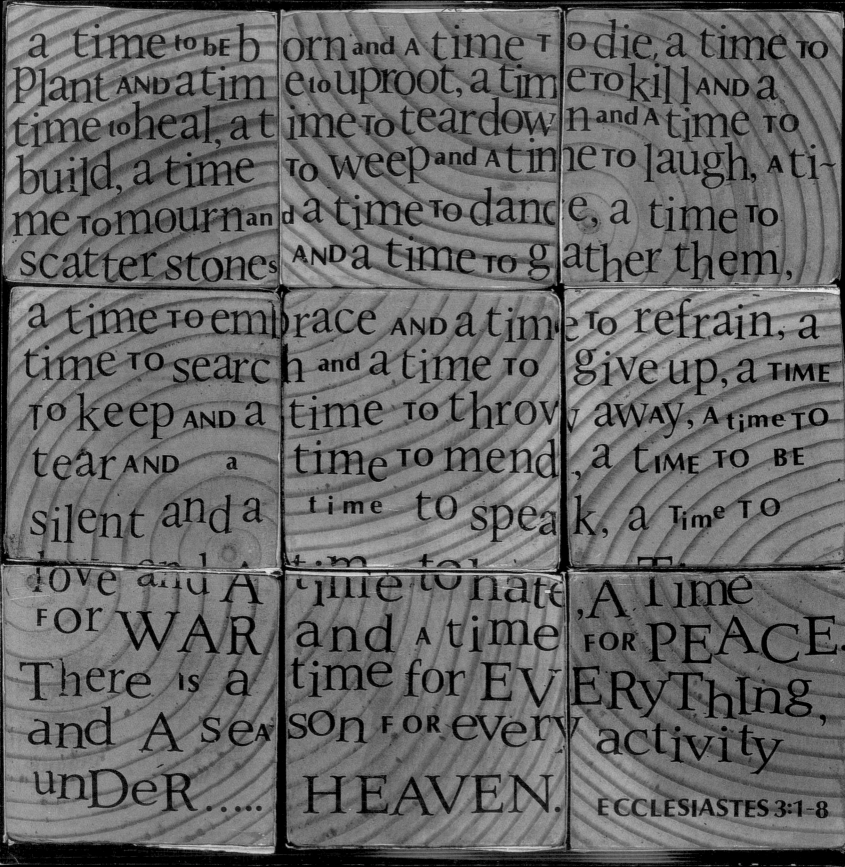

a time to be born and a time to die, a time to plant and a time to uproot, a time to heal, a time to tear down to build, a time to weep and a time to mourn and a time to dance to laugh, a time to scatter stones and a time to gather them, a time to embrace and a time to refrain, a time to search and a time to give up, a time to keep and a time to throw away, a time to tear and a time to mend, a time to be silent and a time to speak, a time to love and a time to hate, a time for WAR and a time for PEACE. There is a time for EVERYThIng, and A season for every activity unDeR..... HEAVEN.

ECCLESIASTES 3:1-8

Brave on the Rocks

New World Library is dedicated to
publishing books and cassettes
that inspire and challenge us to
improve the quality of our lives
and the WORLD.

New World Library books
and tapes are available
in bookstores everywhere.

For a catalog of our complete library
of fine books and cassettes,

Contact:

New World Library
14 Pamaron Way
Novato, CA
94949

Phone: (415) 884-2100
Fax: (415) 884-2199

(800) 972-6657

Catalog requests: Ext. 900
Ordering: Ext. 902

E-mail: escort@nwlib.com
http://www.nwlib.com